PUNCTUATE IT!

COMMAS

BY KATE RIGGS
ILLUSTRATED BY RANDALL ENOS

CREATIVE EDUCATION • CREATIVE PAPERBACKS

Published by Creative Education and Creative Paperbacks
P.O. Box 227, Mankato, Minnesota 56002
Creative Education and Creative Paperbacks are
imprints of The Creative Company
www.thecreativecompany.us

Design and production by Liddy Walseth
Art direction by Rita Marshall
Printed in the United States of America

Illustrations by Randall Enos © 2016

Library of Congress Cataloging-in-Publication Data
Riggs, Kate.
Commas / by Kate Riggs; illustrated by Randall Enos.
p. cm. — (Punctuate it!)
Includes bibliographical references and index.
Summary: An illustrated guide to the punctuation marks known
as commas, including descriptions and examples of how to properly use
them with coordinating conjunctions and as dividers in sentences.
ISBN 978-1-60818-732-4 (hardcover)
ISBN 978-1-62832-328-3 (pbk)
ISBN 978-1-56660-767-4 (eBook)
1. Comma. 2. English language—Punctuation.

PE1450.R518 2016
428.2/3—dc23   2016002550

CCSS: L.1.2; L.2.2; L.3.1, 2, 3, 4, 5; L.4. 1, 2, 3, 4; RI.3.1, 2, 7, 8; RI.4.2, 8

First Edition HC 9 8 7 6 5 4 3 2 1
First Edition PBK 9 8 7 6 5 4 3 2 1

TABLE OF CONTENTS

INTRODUCTION

BETTER TOGETHER

PUNCTUATION PRACTICE

IT'S NECESSARY

PUNCTUATION PRACTICE

SERIAL OFFENDERS

PUNCTUATION PRACTICE

PAUSE FOR A REASON

ACTIVITY: WHERE DID THEY GO?

GLOSSARY | READ MORE
WEBSITE | INDEX

INTRODUCTION

THE HALLWAY IS CROWDED. KIDS PUSH, BACKPACKS SMASH, AND PAPERS FLY. YOU DON'T WANT TO BE LATE FOR CLASS! IF YOU ARE, WHO KNOWS WHAT YOU MIGHT HAVE TO DO? NO NEED TO WORRY. THE BELL RINGS, AND YOU ARE SAFELY IN YOUR SEAT.

BETTER TOGETHER

Commas are everywhere! You may feel as though they're your enemies. But they can be good friends if you know how to use them. Commas divide certain words in a **sentence**. A sentence of one **clause** does not need a comma. However, longer sentences may need at least one comma. Such sentences are sometimes made of two independent clauses.

Independent clauses can stand on their own. They could be full sentences.

Mary likes math. I like science.

What if you wanted to combine those thoughts? You would need more than a comma. You would need a linking word called a coordinating conjunction. You can remember all the coordinating conjunctions by thinking of the word *fanboys*. Each letter stands for one of the conjunctions: **f**or, **a**nd, **n**or, **b**ut, **o**r, **y**et, **s**o.

The best connector for the previous examples would be "but." This word expresses difference. The comma goes before the conjunction.

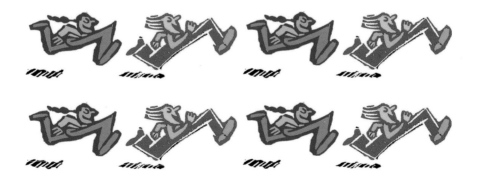

Mary likes math, *but* I like science.

Other sentences have a part that *needs* the independent clause. This is called a dependent clause. It cannot stand on its own. So a dependent clause that comes before an independent one needs a comma.

If a toad hopped into the library, what book would it choose?

PUNCTUATION PRACTICE:

Practice with *fanboys* by thinking of which word makes the most sense as a connector.

Maria finished her work early. She went outside to play.

A: *Maria finished her work early, so she went outside to play.*

You could go on the field trip.
You could write a report.

IT'S NECESSARY

*C*ommas divide sentences in many other ways. They go after an **introductory word** or phrase. They come before or after a name when you're talking directly to that person. Putting a comma in the right place can make a big difference!

Let's study, Cindy.

Let's study Cindy.

In the first sentence, I'm talking to Cindy. I'm letting her know that we should study for a test. In the second sentence,

I'm talking to others. Maybe we're studying a monkey named Cindy for a group project!

A nonrestrictive (or nonessential) phrase tells more about a **subject**. But it is not needed to understand the sentence. Commas always set off nonessential words and phrases.

Harry, thinking he was being funny, made faces at the teacher.

There is an easy test for nonessential phrases. You can take them out and not change the meaning of the sentence.

Harry made faces at the teacher.

Commas are not used with essential, or restrictive, phrases. These groups of words define a sentence's meaning.

The student with the highest grade will win pizza for a week.

Could you rewrite that with commas? No! You need "with the highest grade" to know who qualifies for the free pizza!

PUNCTUATION PRACTICE:

Use a comma to show when a person is being addressed. Sometimes you will need two.

Jack do you know the capital of Idaho?

A: *Jack, do you know the capital of Idaho?*

If you had that class Charlie you would love all the reading.

A: *If you had that class, Charlie, you would love all the reading.*

SERIAL
OFFENDERS

Commas help prevent misunderstandings, so it's a good idea to use them in lists, too. Whenever you have a series of three or more, a comma goes before the conjunction "and." This is called a serial comma.

Olivia, Ann, and Emma sat reading on the bench.

That sentence clearly tells us that there are three girls on the bench. Without commas, we may think there are only two!

Olivia Ann and Emma sat reading on the bench.

PUNCTUATION PRACTICE:

The serial comma is used to link items in a series. Where are commas needed in the following sentence?

Reading science math and music are important subjects.

PAUSE FOR A REASON

*T*here are so many ways to use—and misuse—commas! Always think about why you might need a comma: Is there a conjunction linking two complete thoughts? Is there a phrase that can be removed?

Is there a list of items? Pause to learn the rules, and you will have a powerful punctuation mark at the ready!

WHERE DID THEY GO?

The following paragraph from Kate DiCamillo's *Because of Winn-Dixie* is missing all its commas! Can you figure out where they go? Remember to test for nonessential phrases. Look for conjunctions, too. Hint: there should be seven commas.

The dog went running over to the manager wagging his tail and smiling. He stood up on his hind legs. You could tell that all he wanted to do was get face to face with the manager and thank him for the good time he was having in the produce department but somehow he ended up knocking the manager over. And the manager must have been having a bad day because lying there on the floor right in front of everybody he started to cry. The dog leaned over him real concerned and licked his face.

Answer: The dog went running over to the manager, wagging his tail and smiling. He stood up on his hind legs. You could tell that all he wanted to do was get face to face with the manager and thank him for the good time he was having in the produce department, but somehow he ended up knocking the manager over. And the manager must have been having a bad day, because lying there on the floor, right in front of everybody, he started to cry. The dog leaned over him, real concerned, and licked his face.

GLOSSARY

clause: a unit that makes up a sentence

introductory word: an opening word, such as "yes" or "no," that brings attention to the subject of the rest of the sentence

sentence: a group of words that has a noun as the subject and a verb

subject: the noun that is what or whom the sentence is about

READ MORE

Pulver, Robin. *Punctuation Takes a Vacation.* New York: Holiday House, 2003.

Truss, Lynne. *Eats, Shoots & Leaves: Why, Commas Really Do Make a Difference!* New York: G. P. Putnam's Sons, 2006.

WEBSITE

Grammar Blast

http://www.eduplace.com/kids/hme/k_5/grammar/

Test yourself on what you know about sentences and other punctuation.

Note: Every effort has been made to ensure that the website listed above is suitable for children, that it has educational value, and that it contains no inappropriate material. However, because of the nature of the Internet, it is impossible to guarantee that sites will remain active indefinitely or that their contents will not be altered.

INDEX

conjunctions 8–9, 12, 21, 27, 30

dependent clauses 10–11

direct address 15, 18

essential phrases 17

independent clauses 7–8, 10, 11, 27

introductory words 15

lists 21, 28

nonessential phrases 16, 27, 30

serial commas 21, 25

subjects 16